Sla
the New t

Caryn A Reeder

Professor of New Testament

Westmont College, Santa Barbara CA

GROVE BOOKS LIMITED

RIDLEY HALL RD CAMBRIDGE CB3 9HU

Contents

First Impression September 2019
ISSN 1365-490X
ISBN 978 1 78827 096 0

1 Introduction

> Whoever wishes to become great among you must be your servant, and whoever wishes to be first among you must be slave of all. (Mark 10.43–44)
>
> There is no longer Jew or Greek, there is no longer slave or free, there is no longer male and female; for all of you are one in Christ Jesus. (Gal 3.28)
>
> Slaves, accept the authority of your masters with all deference, not only those who are kind and gentle but also those who are harsh. (1 Pet 2.18)

In the New Testament, slaves guarded doors (Acts 12.13–14), managed their owners' wealth (Matt 25.14–30), prepared feasts and more (Luke 15.23). Slaves, freed slaves and slave owners worshipped together in early church communities (1 Cor 7.21–23; 1 Tim 6.1–2; Phile 15–16). The imagery of slavery described a person's relationship to sin and to God (John 8.33–36; Rom 6.16–20).

These references help us see just how common slavery was in the world of the earliest Christians. The Roman Empire was a slave society. According to Gaius, a second-century Roman lawyer, 'The principal distinction made by the law of nature is this, that all human beings are either free people or slaves' (*Institutes* 1.9). 'Slave,' 'freed slave' and 'freeborn' were fundamental categories of identity. A person's status determined their legal rights (or lack of rights), their ability to protect their own bodies against abuse and their capacity for social honour.

Although slavery was pervasive in the world of the New Testament, it is often invisible to us. When a story or letter does not identify a person as 'slave' or 'free,' we do not ask about their status, or how that status affected their daily life. Therefore, we do not wonder what the gospel message meant for slaves, freed slaves and slave owners. For instance, how did the earliest Christians experience the unity of slaves and free people in Christ? How did they understand the exhortations for Christians to humble themselves and serve (or 'be enslaved to') each other? What did freedom in Christ mean for Christians who were enslaved to human owners?

In this book, we will explore slavery in the Roman Empire as a context for interpreting the New Testament. Learning about slavery helps us understand what daily life was like for our ancestors in faith. Learning about Roman slavery also helps us see how complicated and difficult it must have been for Jesus' followers to put their new faith into practice.

The stories and letters in the New Testament interact with the realities of slavery in complex ways. When we interpret key New Testament texts in the context of Roman slavery, we might find new challenges to our own assumptions about the world and our own lives as disciples of Jesus.

Defining Slavery in the Roman Empire

The Roman Empire was a slave society. This conclusion is based on the percentage of the population that was enslaved, the importance of slavery for the imperial economy and productivity and the place of slavery in Rome's social hierarchies.[1] These three factors characterized the system of slavery in the world of Jesus and his earliest followers.

Population

In the mid-first century, Pliny the Elder complained that Roman households were full of 'legions of slaves'—so many that slave owners needed one slave whose job it was to keep track of all the others (*Natural History* 33.26). Scholars estimate that around ten per cent of the entire population of the Empire was enslaved, with significantly higher percentages in Asia Minor, Gaul, Italy and the city of Rome itself. Most Roman households owned slaves, from just a few in a poor household to hundreds or even thousands on a wealthy estate.[2]

It is no surprise, then, to find slaves and slave owners in the stories and letters of the New Testament. It is likely that many (or even most) people we meet in the New Testament were slaves, had been slaves or owned slaves.

The Economy and Productivity

There are different systems of slavery. One type, debt slavery, was practised in biblical Israel, ancient Greece and the Roman Republic. In debt slavery, people sell themselves or their children into slavery for financial reasons. Comparable practices are mentioned in the Old Testament, with various restrictions (Exod 21.7; Lev 25.39–43; Neh 5.4–5).

By the time of the New Testament, debt slavery was uncommon in the Roman Empire.[3] The primary system of slavery in ancient Greece and Rome was chattel slavery. Aristotle defined chattel slavery as total ownership of a human life: 'The slave isn't just the slave of a master, but belongs to him completely…A human being belongs to another when he is a piece of property as well as being human' (*Politics* 6–7). Chattel slaves were living, breathing property, tools for slave owners to use for their own benefit.[4]

The concept of complete ownership drove the New Testament's metaphors of enslavement to sin and to God (Rom 6.16–23). As Paul told the Corinthians, 'You were bought for a price'—and being owned by God demanded obedience and faithfulness to God (1 Cor 6.19–20).

To identify slaves as property made slavery an important economic concern. The slave trade was a significant source of revenue for the Roman Empire.[5] In 1 Tim 1.9–11 and Rev 18.11–13, the exploitation of human life for personal and imperial economic gain is condemned. Slavery was also a major mode of production, from individual households to agricultural estates to the imperial government.[6] Jesus's parables in Matt 13.24–30 and Luke 17.7–8, the story of the slave girl of Philippi in Acts 16 and the instructions to slaves in 1 Tim 6.1–2 reflect the concerns of slave productivity.

The Social Hierarchy of Rome

In Roman society, being fully human required self-discipline and control over others. The value placed on personal power marked wealthy, aristocratic men who commanded in the military, governed the provinces or sat in the Senate as model Romans. The most ideal human in the Empire was the emperor, the figure of power at the top of the hierarchy.[7]

Wealthy, aristocratic women also exercised social power, though their power was not necessarily of the same kind or extent as the men in their families. Poor, freeborn men, women and children were lower on the hierarchy. They rarely had power over others outside the household. Freed slaves were lower still. Slaves were barely human at all, precisely because they lacked power over their own persons.[8]

In the Roman social hierarchy, an individual's status as a slave, a freed slave or a freeborn person was an essential element of identity. In some ways, this status mattered more than whether a person was rich or poor, or male or female. Jesus's exhortation to the twelve disciples in Mark 10.43–44 and Paul's proclamation in Gal 3.28 challenged the social hierarchy, displacing power as a defining mark of humanity.

Experiencing Slavery in the Roman Empire

> Cato owned many house slaves, and usually bought those prisoners of war who were young and still capable of being reared and trained like young dogs or colts. (Plutarch, *Cato the Elder* 21.1)

Slaves sometimes had close relationships with their owners. They had the potential for education, important positions in wealthy families, and freedom. But, as Plutarch's story of Cato suggests, slavery was not a benign or beneficial system.

Freeborn Romans compared slaves to animals and young children, lacking the capacity for reason and self-control. They also judged slaves to be immoral, with a tendency to laziness, theft and murder. As a consequence, slave owners like Cato trained and controlled their slaves through physical violence.

Unlike slavery in the Americas, the Roman system of slavery was not racial. Many slaves were foreigners, brought into the Empire by war or by the slave trade, but they were as likely to be German or British as African. But while the Romans were not racist in their slavery, they dehumanized slaves just as much as in the American systems. Keith Bradley sums up the Roman system of slavery like this:

> It is a historical, objective reality that slavery was an evil, violent and brutalizing institution that the Romans themselves, across a vast interval of time and space, consciously chose to maintain, for which they themselves were responsible, whose justification they never seriously questioned and for which no apology or exoneration can now be offered.[9]

Slaves had no legal rights, personal honour or bodily autonomy. They had few protections against cruelty, abuse or neglect. For one freed slave, Publilius Syrus, 'It is beautiful to die instead of being degraded as a slave' (*Sentences* 489). The Romans identified slavery as a living death.[10]

The horrors of slavery are clear in New Testament references to the abuse of slaves (for instance Matt 18.23–34; Mark 12.2–5; 1 Pet 2.18–20). Even when such horrors are not in focus, though, we should not forget the humiliation, powerlessness and the potential for violence in the lives of the slaves in the early church.

In this book, we will explore the realities and imagery of slavery and freedom in the Roman Empire. Chapter two addresses the daily experiences of slavery, and chapter three addresses how slaves might gain their freedom. Chapter four examines metaphors of slavery. These different concerns provide a fuller context for interpreting slavery and freedom, the lives of slaves and slave owners and the expectation of mutual enslavement in the New Testament.

As in this chapter, I will refer to some Greek and Roman sources to explain what slavery was like in the ancient world. If you are interested in reading more, you can find these sources online.[11] There are also several good collections of translated texts on slavery as part of life in the Roman world.[12]

2 The Daily Experiences of Slavery

> To Titus Flavius Euschemon, freed slave of Augustus, who had been secretary for correspondence and also procurator of the Jewish poll tax. Flavia Aphrodisia set this up for her ex-owner and husband, who well deserved it.
>
> To Italia, dressmaker of Cocceia Phyllis. She lived twenty years. Acastus, her fellow slave, paid for this tombstone because she was poor.[13]

Titus Flavius Euschemon was well educated. He worked in the government, sharing in the status and authority of his owner, Emperor Augustus. He gained his own freedom. He was able to free and marry his own slave, Flavia Aphrodisia.

The slaves in the second inscription above had more mundane lives. Italia was a seamstress. Acastus, a slave belonging to the same owner, said Italia was poor (though Acastus himself had enough money to purchase an inscription). Italia died as a slave at a young age.

These two funerary inscriptions indicate just how different the experience of slavery might be for slaves, depending on their age, sex, education and the wealth of their owners. In this chapter, we will survey the ways a person might become a slave, the work of slavery, slaves' living conditions and the treatment slaves could expect in their daily lives. We only catch glimpses of slaves in the New Testament. This chapter attempts to understand what their everyday lives may have been like.

Becoming a Slave

Some slaves in the Roman Empire were born into slavery, but freeborn people also became slaves through capture in war or less legal means. The experience of slavery was very different for people who were born and raised to be slaves and those who became enslaved later in their lives.

Rome's wars brought many new slaves into the Empire, as Jesus warned in Luke 21.24. Josephus, a Jewish historian who wrote about the Jewish revolt against Rome in the first century, claimed that the Roman army captured

97,000 slaves in Galilee and Judea—so many that the slave market was glutted (*Jewish War* 6.384, 420).

For people who had been free before their capture, the loss of rights over their own bodies added to the trauma of war.[14] The same would be true for people kidnapped by pirates or brigands in deserted places around the Empire.[15] The fall from the honour of freedom into the humiliation of slavery was so distressing that, in many stories, the newly enslaved committed suicide. This is the reason Josephus gave for the mass suicide at Masada on the eve of the Roman victory over the Jews there (*Jewish War* 7.380–387).

The fall from into slavery was so distressing that, in many stories, the newly enslaved committed suicide

The philosopher Seneca observed that a newly enslaved person might be too slow to keep up with the owner's carriage, too accustomed to sleep to keep watch through the night, too weak to manage difficult labor, and too proud to work at dishonourable tasks (*On Anger* 3.29.1–2). Captives of war or kidnapping faced drastic changes in their daily lives. Their new owners renamed them and they often had to learn a new language and social customs. The captives in Jesus' warning in Luke 21.24 survived the destruction of Jerusalem, but their lives would never be the same.

Child exposure was another source of slaves. If a family could not afford to raise a child in addition to providing for the rest of the household, they left the baby (especially if it was a girl) in a public garbage dump or on the street. Stories of the exposure of infants in the ancient world emphasized the difficulty of this decision for parents (for instance Ovid, *Metamorphosis* 9.666). Many exposed babies died, but they could also be taken and raised as slaves.[16]

Finally, natural reproduction was a significant source of slaves. A baby born to a slave woman was a slave. The father's status was irrelevant, and in fact many slave children would have been fathered by the slaves' owners. Because natural reproduction was such a common source for slaves, it is possible that many of the slaves in New Testament stories and letters were born into slavery.

Such slaves often identified themselves as 'houseborn' in funerary inscriptions, and they were sometimes described with affection by owners (Pliny the Elder, *Natural History* 22.44). Any affection, however, does not change the fact that these people were enslaved, and that their owners, however caring, had absolute authority over them. Bradley suggests that houseborn slaves were more desirable than captive slaves not for emotional reasons, but because they were born into their position. They never knew another reality.[17]

Daily Life

> Who among you would say to your slave who has just come in from plowing or tending sheep in the field, 'Come here at once and take your place at the table'? Would you not rather say to him, 'Prepare supper for me, put on your apron and serve me while I eat and drink; later you may eat and drink'? Do you thank the slave for doing what was commanded? So you also, when you have done all that you were ordered to do, say, 'We are worthless slaves; we have done only what we ought to have done!' (Luke 17.7–10)

Jesus' questions to his disciples in Luke 17.7–10 assumed that slaves worked hard through the day at a variety of tasks, all on their owners' behalf. There was no need for gratitude on the owner's part because slaves were only tools for the owner to use (more like hammers or refrigerators than waiting staff or house cleaners). Jesus's final question turned the expectations of slavery upside down by identifying the disciples as slaves (see chapter four), but otherwise the parable reflected Roman custom.

In very wealthy homes, some young child slaves became objects of affection to their owners, pampered and played with (sometimes in disturbingly sexualized ways).[18] Most child slaves did not have what we would consider a childhood. Rather, they began work as soon as their bodies were capable of simple tasks. The first-century writer Columella commented that slaves on agricultural estates were 'hardened to farm work from infancy' (*On Agriculture* 1.8.2), and contracts for apprenticeships to weavers and other skilled workers record young ages for slaves.

Slaves continued working until death—which might come at a younger age than for a free person, considering the difficult conditions of slavery. Unless a slave gained freedom as a gift of their owner, old age did not mean automatic retirement from labour. In fact, in some cases slave owners stopped providing for elderly slaves: 'Cato thought that when the slaves got older, they should be got rid of not fed when they were no longer useful' (Plutarch, *Cato the Elder* 4.4). Plutarch disapproved of this custom, but it is understandable within the Roman definition of slaves as tools for the owners' benefit.

Slaves in towns and cities engaged in a variety of jobs. In a household with hundreds of slaves, each slave might have just one responsibility: guarding the door; cooking meals; weeding the courtyard garden; running errands; hairdressing; or making clothing, for instance. The slave woman with a spirit of divination in Acts 16.16–19 is an example of the specializations of slavery. In poorer households, slaves might have multiple tasks, from skilled labour to cooking and cleaning (as in Luke 17.7–10).

Some slaves in a wealthy household might be very well educated, working as secretaries or running businesses for their owners. Slaves like these starred in Jesus's parables (Matt 25.14–30; Luke 16.1–8). Slave women nursed freeborn and enslaved infants, and slaves also educated their owners' children.[19] In fact, many teachers in Roman schools were freed slaves. Owners also commonly hired their male and female slaves out as prostitutes (comparable to sex trafficking today).[20]

Many teachers in Roman schools were freed slaves

In a wealthy urban household, some slaves shared small rooms as sleeping quarters. Others slept in storerooms, hallways or, for slaves who might be needed in the night, in their owners' bedrooms.[21] Slaves of wealthy owners were often well dressed, since their appearance showed off their owners' status.[22] In a poorer household, slaves did not necessarily have their own living space, decent clothing or adequate food.

Medical care depended on the owners' decision. Owners who valued their slaves might seek treatment, as in the case of the centurion who asked Jesus to heal his slave in Luke 7.2–3. However, as in the story about Cato above, there are also reports of slaves being abandoned if they were too sick or old to work.

Jesus' parables sometimes mentioned slaves in agricultural work (Matt 13.27; Luke 17.7–10). In rural areas, slaves grew vegetables and grain, tended vineyards and cared for animals. Slaves on large agricultural estates often had more independence since they lived away from the daily supervision of their owners. The absence of the owner, however, also meant an absence of care, so rural slaves might not have appropriate shelter, clothing or food.[23]

> Nowadays those agricultural operations are performed by slaves with fettered ankles and by the hands of malefactors with branded faces. (Pliny the Elder, *Natural History* 18.21)

Slave owners feared the independence of rural slaves. They sometimes chained or abused slaves on agricultural estates to keep them under control.

Other slaves fell outside the urban / rural division. Like the unnamed centurion in Luke 7.2 and Cornelius in Acts 10.7, soldiers in the Roman military took slaves on their military postings and to war. Josephus says the Romans trained military slaves like soldiers (*Jewish War* 3.69–70). Gladiators who fought to the death for the entertainment of Roman audiences were often slaves or criminals.

Contractors who carried out building projects like roads or aqueducts owned gangs of slaves to work on these projects; little is known of this experience of slavery. Other slaves worked in mines under very poor conditions and abuse. Diodorus Siculus said these slaves 'wear out their bodies both by day and by night in the diggings under the earth, dying in large numbers because of the exceptional hardships they endure' (*Library* 5.38). These slaves do not appear in the stories or letters of the New Testament, and it is hard to imagine how the earliest Christians could have shared the gospel with them.

Personal Experience

Slaves who were part of the same household lived, worked and relaxed together. In funerary inscriptions, slaves referred to each other as family members and friends. Funerary inscriptions also indicate enduring relationships between slaves and slave owners.

We see such relationships in Acts. Rhoda, a slave, knew Peter well enough to recognize him immediately when he unexpectedly came to the door. She was one of a few members of the church in Jerusalem to be recorded by name (Acts 12.12–15). Two slaves and a soldier escorted Peter to Cornelius's house and, therefore, these slaves were instrumental in the preaching of the gospel to Gentiles (Acts 10.7–8). When the head of the household like Cornelius or Lydia became a Christian, all the members of the household—a group which included slaves—were baptized (Acts 10.44–48; 16.15, 33).

While slaves were part of their owners' households, under Roman law they could not legally marry. However, slaves might form relationships akin to marriage with each other and have children together. In the parable in Matt 18.24–25, a slave had a wife and children. But the owner's actions indicated that he owned his slave's wife and children. Owners permitted or forbade their slaves' relationships. Owners also arranged or enforced relationships in order to encourage procreation and additions to the numbers of slaves in a household.[24]

Being in a slave marriage did not protect a slave's body from others

Being in a slave marriage did not protect a slave's body from others. Slaves had no right to refuse their owners' sexual advances. Seneca the Elder claimed that unchastity was a necessity for slaves (*Controversies* 4, preface 10), and Plutarch said that husbands honoured their wives by using slaves for sex (*Marriage Advice* 16). Numerous stories, letters, and poetry from the Roman world indicate the expectation of the sexual availability of male and female slaves of all ages, both within private households and as public prostitutes, to their (male) owners.[25]

In 1 Cor 6.15–20, Paul prohibited Christians from visiting prostitutes. This prohibition may suggest that Christian slave owners should also not use their slaves for sex. But since the sexual use of slaves was not at all immoral by Roman standards, scholars like Jennifer Glancy wonder if Christian slave owners would have stopped participating in such practices.[26] This specific situation is not as clearly addressed in the New Testament as we might expect in light of the frequency (and acceptance) with which Roman slave owners used their slaves for sex.

Notably, in 1 Cor 6.16–20 Paul did not address the prostitutes or slaves themselves. Slaves had no rights over their own bodies—they could not 'flee immorality' (1 Cor 6.18, author's translation). The consistent New Testament expectations of sexual morality would have been complicated for slaves who endured sexual exploitation.

> You say, Rufus, that your rabbit has not been cooked well, and you call for a whip. (Martial, *Epigrams* 3.94)

In addition to sexual exploitation, slaves could expect violence as part of their daily lives, as we see in Jesus' parables (Mark 12.2–5; Luke 12.45–48). Owners beat and flogged slaves in order to train them to obedience and to punish them. Since slaves were personal property, owners even had the right to execute their slaves for wrongdoing. However, social honour placed some limits on slave owners. When one owner ordered a slave to be fed to lampreys, the emperor freed the slave and had the fishpond filled in (Seneca, *On Anger* 3.40.2).

In 1 Pet 2.18–25, Peter assumed that Christian slaves regularly faced violence and abuse, even if they were obedient to their (non-Christian) owners. Slaves had few options in situations of abuse. Peter therefore redefined the experience as Christlike suffering. In 1 Pet 2.21, slaves with no power over their own persons represented the ultimate followers of Jesus, who was also unjustly beaten.

Slavery in the New Testament Household Codes

Peter's instructions to slaves in 1 Pet 2.18–25 are an example of the household codes of the Greco-Roman world. These behavioural guides were usually addressed to the eldest male of the household, giving him the responsibility of teaching his subordinates—his wife, children and slaves—to be obedient, honourable members of society.

Several New Testament letters incorporated instructions like these. The earliest Christians were persecuted for refusing to worship the ancestral gods, proclaiming a king besides the emperor, and undermining foundational cultural values (Acts 16.20–23; 17.6–7; 19.23–41; 1 Pet 2.12; 3.16; 4.1–4). In this context, the New Testament household codes encouraged Christians to behave in ways that non-Christians would see as honourable and good so that, as 1 Tim 6.1 said, 'the name of God and the teaching may not be blasphemed.'

In line with Roman expectation, then, Eph 6.5–8, Col 3.22–25, 1 Tim 6.1–2 and 1 Pet 2.18–25 instructed slaves to be obedient to their owners. Slaves should devote themselves to the work of slavery, whether their owners were watching or not (and, for 1 Peter, even if they were beaten despite their good behaviour). Instructions like these would surely have been acceptable in the Roman world.

It may be surprising to readers today that New Testament authors did not ask slave owners to free their slaves (an issue addressed in the next chapter). There are, nonetheless, some important differences from the Greco-Roman household codes. First, unlike the Greco-Roman examples, the New Testament texts directly addressed the slaves themselves. The direct address gave the slaves their own agency, making them—and not their owners—responsible for their own behaviour.[27] Secondly, in Eph 6.9 and Col 4.1, Paul commanded slave owners not to threaten their slaves, but rather treat them with 'justice and equality.' Like the instructions given to husbands and fathers in Eph 5.25–33 and 6.4 and Col 3.19 and 21, the instructions to slave owners limited their power over vulnerable members of their households. Thirdly, Paul reminded slaves that their true owner is God—and slave owners are also owned by God. In these ways, the New Testament household codes challenged Greco-Roman social norms.

3

Freedom and Slavery

There is only one clear, unambiguous reference to freedom for slaves in the New Testament: the Synagogue of the Freedmen (that is, freed slaves) in Acts 6.9. Beyond this reference, the two texts that are most important for the question of slaves' freedom in the New Testament are 1 Cor 7.21–23 and Paul's letter to Philemon. In both cases, the interpretation of the texts is strongly debated. In this chapter, we will explore what freedom and slavery meant in the Roman world and how slaves might become free as context for the interpretation of these contentious texts.

Freedom and Slavery in Roman Thought

For the Romans, as we have seen, the state of being free was valuable and honourable, while slavery was a living death. But despite the value of freedom, the philosopher Seneca argued that in some sense, all people are slaves. To be human is to be enslaved to something or someone (*Letters* 47). He also claimed that actual slaves possessed a fundamental freedom of the mind despite their enslavement (*On Benefits* 3.19–20).

While he explored these ideas, though, Seneca owned slaves, and he frequently used the harsh experiences of slavery as examples in his writings. As Keith Bradley comments, philosophers like Seneca did not bring practical changes to the system of slavery.[28]

Slave owners sometimes celebrated the granting of freedom to particular slaves (Cicero, *Letters* 16.16). In other cases, they celebrated enslavement:

> This tomb is a sufficient resting place for wise Bithynis, a slave of worthy masters…For I did not strive for freedom, but I was well rewarded, and I have this memorial which is more enduring than liberty.[29]

This funerary inscription, likely to have been written by the slave's owners, upheld the servitude of the slave woman Bithynis. It suggested that a desire for freedom from slavery was less worthy than dying as a slave.

Despite slave owners' attempts to define slavery as a good, virtuous pursuit, slaves across the Roman world desired freedom and the status it brought. Slaves could seek freedom officially through manumission, and illegally by running away. Different kinds of freedom had different consequences for a slave's life.

Manumission

Manumission is the official term for setting a slave free. The formal process of manumission was carefully controlled under Roman law. Slave owners could free only a certain number of slaves at a time, since freeing slaves decreased the value of the property for heirs. Slaves freed in this way were given Roman citizenship. Informal manumission was less strictly regulated, but slaves freed in this way did not gain citizenship.[30]

Some slaves managed to purchase their own manumission by means of *peculium*, money that resourceful, privileged slaves earned from tips, odd jobs or small businesses. This money belonged, like the slaves themselves, to their owners. However, owners traditionally allowed slaves to use their *peculium* to buy their own lives. Alternatively, a relation or friend could purchase a slave's freedom.

Owners sometimes chose to give slaves freedom in recognition of lifelong servitude, a close personal relationship, or the slave's personal merits (education, skill or performing an extraordinary service for the owner). Such manumissions sometimes occurred while the owner was still living, but most happened at the owner's death. To set slaves free by will brought honour to the deceased for their generosity.[31]

Freedom brought many benefits. A freed slave had the legal right to own property and make a will. Children born after manumission were freeborn by status. Freed slaves gained the capacity for social honour and bodily autonomy. Manumission did not free a slave from all obligations, however, as this early first-century contract indicates:

> On the following conditions Sophrona, acting with the consent of her son Sosandros, sets free the female house-born slave named Onasiphoron...Onasiphoron is to remain with Sophrona for the whole period of Sophrona's life, doing whatever she is ordered to do without giving cause for complaint. If she does not do so, then Sophrona is to have the power to punish her in whatever way she wishes to. And Onasiphoron is to give Sosandros a child. (*Fouilles de Delphes* 3,6, No. 36)[32]

By law, freed slaves had to act with honour and respect to their former owners. They had to work for their former owners a certain number of days a year. They had financial obligations to their owners, and potentially owed their owners new slave bodies (their own children).

Manumission was somewhat common for urban household slaves, and we are likely to have met some freed slaves in the New Testament without knowing it. But many slaves would not have had the opportunity for manumission, including uneducated or untrained household slaves, rural slaves and slaves who worked in mines or on public works projects. Moreover, by the time a slave was freed, they were likely to be elderly, or physically worn out from years of labour, bodily abuse and the emotional stress of slavery. As Bradley argues, the system of manumission advantaged the owners of slaves, rather than the slaves themselves.[33]

Freedom Without Manumission

> We still believe today that by their prayers our Vestal Virgins can make slaves who have run away but haven't yet got out of Rome stay where they are. (Pliny the Elder, *Natural History* 28.3)

Roman authors regularly mentioned runaway slaves, and there are numerous surviving advertisements for runaway slaves. These facts suggest that slaves frequently tried to find their own freedom by escape.[34] There was no obvious way to tell if someone was free or slave. Moreover, slaves sometimes worked on their own, without observation, inside and outside the household. In these circumstances, running away must have been tempting.

Because slaves were property, runaway slaves stole themselves. Anyone who protected a runaway was also guilty of theft under Roman law (*Digest* 11.4.1). If caught, a runaway slave was beaten. To prevent future attempts at escape, iron collars with inscriptions listing the owner's name were permanently attached to the slave's neck, or the slave was branded on the forehead with an F for fugitive. These punishments were also intended to discourage other slaves from stealing their own freedom. But for the slaves, the punishments may not have been any worse than the state of enslavement.[35]

A second, more drastic alternative to manumission was murder. Roman sources record multiple stories of slaves who attempted to gain their freedom by killing their owners. Pliny the Younger told of slaves beating their owner to death. This slave owner was apparently cruel and abusive, but Pliny commented that even kindness to slaves did not prevent such criminal behaviour (*Letters* 3.14).[36]

A third alternative to manumission was the slave's death. Some slaves chose to commit suicide to escape abusive treatment or to avoid harsh punishment (Seneca, *Epistles* 4.4). Many more slaves died in slavery from illness, injury, the consequences of malnutrition, and physical exhaustion and old age.

1 Corinthians 7.21-23

In 1 Cor 7.12–20, Paul recommended that Christians married to non-Christians should remain married, the circumcised should stay circumcised, and the uncircumcised should stay uncircumcised: 'Let each of you remain in the condition in which you were called.' In vv 21–23, Paul expanded this message to the situation of slaves.

Paul began by saying that the state of enslavement should not be a worry or concern to slaves. He then added, if a slave could become free, they should 'make use' of it. Some interpreters suggest that, similar to the cases of marriage and circumcision, v 21 means slaves should stay enslaved. The NRSV translation reflects this interpretation: 'Even if you can gain your freedom, make use of your present condition now more than ever.' Slaves should use their enslavement for good, even if they had the opportunity to become free.

A problem with this interpretation is that, as we have seen, slaves did not have a choice in their own enslavement. Manumission was the right of slave owners. If Paul thought that slaves should stay enslaved, refusing any opportunity for freedom, his instructions would make little sense. Perhaps, then, v 21 means that, if slaves have the opportunity for freedom, they should make use of it (as in the NIV translation). They were 'bought with a price' (that is, Christ's death), and they should not enslave themselves to humans.[37]

Paul's message in 1 Cor 7.21–22 is very clear on one point. In Christ, people enslaved by human owners are free, and people who think they are free are in fact owned by God. This message has practical consequences for Christian slaves and slave owners. First, that slaves served God allowed them to reinterpret their inescapable daily experience as honourable and life-giving (as in Eph 6.5–8 and Col 3.22–25). Moreover, when slaves faced deprivation, humiliating work and abuse, they could remember that they were free in Christ. Secondly, that slave owners were themselves owned by God meant that they had no innate honour or privilege. They were slaves, just like the slaves they owned—and so they should treat their slaves well (as in Eph 6.9 and Col 4.1).

Philemon and Onesimus

Paul's letter to Philemon, Apphia, Archippus and the church that gathered in their house is important to any discussion of freedom and slavery in the New Testament. However, this short letter does not give us enough evidence to understand the situation fully. Precisely what Paul wanted Philemon to do is a matter of debate.

Most interpreters agree that Onesimus was a slave belonging to Philemon. Onesimus did something that harmed Philemon (v 18). Onesimus then somehow met Paul in prison and became a Christian (v 10). Paul sent Onesimus back to Philemon (v 12). He asked Philemon to welcome Onesimus as if he were Paul himself, to charge anything that Onesimus owed Philemon to Paul, and to prepare a guest room for Paul (vv 17–19, 22).

Some interpreters think that Onesimus ran away from Philemon.[38] If this was the way Onesimus wronged Philemon, then he owed Philemon his life. In this case, Paul's reminder that Philemon owed Paul his own life gently questioned Philemon's ownership of Onesimus. Paul also claimed Onesimus as his own child, taking on the authority of a father over Onesimus (v 12). Perhaps Paul expected Philemon to set Onesimus free because he was no longer a slave—he was a 'beloved brother' (v 16).

Other interpreters suggest that Philemon sent Onesimus to take supplies or carry a message to Paul, but Onesimus overstayed his leave (or stole something from Philemon). Onesimus would expect punishment for whatever he did when he returned home. If this is the story behind the letter, then Paul attempted to smooth over the situation and restore the relationship between the slave and slave owner. Manumission is not part of this interpretation. As in all early church communities, Onesimus could be both a slave and a beloved brother in Christ at the same time.

Onesimus could be both a slave and a beloved brother in Christ at the same time

The questions surrounding the interpretation of this letter indicate the complex practical considerations of slaves and slave owners in the early church. The earliest Christians lived in a slave society. Freeing slaves was limited by law, and overly harsh or overly generous treatment of slaves affected owners' social honour and status. To work out the theological truths of freedom in Christ and enslavement to God within the realities of life in the Roman Empire was not easy.[39]

Manumission, Abolition and the New Testament

Slavery was fundamental to life in the Roman Empire. Perhaps because of this, there is no command in the New Testament for Christian slave owners to free their slaves. Instead, Paul and Peter instructed Christian slaves to be good slaves, obeying their human owners as if they were obeying God (Eph 6.5–8; 1 Pet 2.18–21).

The New Testament household codes, among other texts, were used by supporters of slavery in the Americas to counter the abolitionist movement.[40] Slave owners argued that slavery was a natural part of the social order of the world. They also claimed that the enslavement of Africans and indigenous peoples was for their own good. According to white slave owners, races they saw as inferior would become civilized through slavery.[41]

Opponents of slavery also drew on biblical evidence. They pointed to the refrain that repeats through the Old Testament: God saved Israel from slavery (Exod 20.2; Ps 81.10; Jer 34.13). Paul proclaimed that in Christ, there was no slave or free (1 Cor 12.13; Gal 3.27–28; Col 3.11). For Christian slaves and abolitionists, texts like these demanded the abolition of slavery.[42]

> Slavery's children entered history from below: from their straitened vantage they came to see in the holy Scriptures that God grants victory to the unlikeliest people—people like themselves—and by the unlikeliest means. The Bible privileges those without privilege and honours those without honour...(A Callahan, *The Talking Book*)[43]

New Testament authors did not demand the end of slavery as a social and economic system. However, they did critique the core assumptions of Roman slavery: the dehumanizing of people made in God's image; abusiveness as a matter of course; and the very idea of ownership over human lives. As in Rev 18.11–13, slavery and the slave trade brought divine judgment on the Roman Empire.

The message of mutual submission is fundamental to discipleship in the New Testament.

> For you were called to freedom, brothers and sisters; only do not use your freedom as an opportunity for self-indulgence, but through love become slaves to one another. (Gal 5.13)

We should not overlook how radical this message would have sounded in the early church, in the midst of Rome's slave society. Even if the New Testament authors did not proclaim the end of slavery, their redefinition of freedom and slavery challenged the fundamental social values of their day.[44]

How might these messages sound today? The New Testament asks us to question our own structures of power and status. Even if we consider slavery to be illegal, are there ways we nonetheless fail to recognize the basic humanity of the people around us? Are there ways that Christian leaders could do better at giving up their power and privilege for the sake of their congregations? If we listen carefully, the subtle challenges to the Roman system of slavery in the New Testament encourage those with power and privilege to give up their privileges for the sake of the less privileged.

4 Metaphors and Similes of Slavery in the New Testament

In the second century BC, Prusias, king of Bithynia, made an alliance with the Roman Republic. He wanted to shore up his own power and protect his kingdom against war-hungry neighbours. Prusias' decision to seek this alliance was a smart political move. But for the historian Polybius, Prusias' manner as he approached the Roman Senate was humiliating:

> On entering the senate house Prusias stood in the doorway facing the members, and putting both his hands on the ground he bowed his head to the ground in adoration of the threshold and the seated senators, with the words, 'Hail, you saviour gods,' making it impossible for anyone after him to surpass him in unmanliness, womanishness, and slavishness. (Polybius, *Histories* 30.18.5)

In Rome's slave society, slavishness was a slur. 'Merely to label someone or something servile or slavish was to project the disgrace of slavery, and the demeanour of the slave was to be avoided at all costs.'[45] To refer to a person (or an entire people group) as slavish was demeaning and dehumanizing. Cicero describes the Syrians and Jews as peoples 'born for slavery' in this sense (*On the Consular Provinces* 5.10).

Consider what the following New Testament texts might mean in this context:

> Whoever wishes to become great among you must be your servant, and whoever wishes to be first among you must be slave of all. (Mark 10.43–44)
>
> Now present your members as slaves to righteousness for sanctification. (Rom 6.19)
>
> [Christ Jesus] emptied himself, taking the form of a slave, being born in human likeness. And being found in human form, he humbled himself and became obedient to the point of death—even death on a cross. (Phil 2.7–8)

In these texts, the imagery and expectations of slavery describe who Jesus was and, therefore, what it meant to be a disciple of Jesus. For Christians who understood slavishness as an insult, this foundational message must have been shocking and difficult to comprehend.

Like a Slave

In Mark's gospel, Jesus' disciples frequently misunderstood his teachings. In particular, they did not seem able to grasp the idea that Jesus was going to Jerusalem to be killed. Like most Jews in Jesus' day, the disciples expected for the messiah to be a conquering king. Peter even rebuked Jesus for saying he would suffer and die (Mark 8.31–33).

In Mark 9.33–37, just after Jesus' second announcement of his coming death, the disciples began arguing about which of them was the greatest disciple. Jesus told them, 'Whoever wants to be first must be last of all and servant of all' (v 35). In this story, Jesus used a child as an example for the disciples. Soon after, in Mark 10.13–16, Jesus explicitly identified children as a model for discipleship.

Children in Jesus' day were socially insignificant.[46] Like slaves, children were under the authority of others (their parents). In fact, the Greek word *pais* can mean either child or slave. But according to Jesus, in order to enter the kingdom of God, his followers must become like a little child. They must give up their own desire for social significance and autonomy to be dependent on and obedient to God.

Despite the repetition, James and John still did not understand Jesus's message. So, in Mark 10.35–44, they approached Jesus with a request. When Jesus claimed his kingdom, they wanted to rule with him, seated right beside his throne. This request upset the other ten disciples. Jesus then said to his disciples,

> You know that among the Gentiles those whom they recognize as their rulers lord it over them, and their great ones are tyrants over them. But it is not so among you; but whoever wishes to become great among you must be your servant, and whoever wishes to be first among you must be slave of all. (Mark 10.42–44)

Jesus suggested that the rulers of the Gentile world, including the Romans, used their power and privilege to exploit their subjects. Instead of following this model, Jesus wanted the disciples to give up personal rights and privileges for the sake of others: 'For the Son of Man came not to be served but to serve, and to give his life a ransom for many' (Mark 10.45).

C Conway argues that Mark's message of servanthood had parallels in Greek and Roman thought. Good rulers should serve their subjects.[47] I wonder, however, if Jesus' statements were more radical than the Greek or Roman parallels. For the Romans, authority over self and others was the mark of true humanity. To give up one's privilege was correspondingly dishonourable.

The series of stories in Mark's gospel identified Jesus as the ultimate slave, giving up even his right to life.[48] The disciples, men who apparently expected to gain power and status through their association with Jesus, should instead identify with the powerless. They must become like children and slaves. Jesus' message stood in opposition to the Roman values of power, control and honour.

All four gospels include this message. In Matt 23.6–12, Jesus discouraged the disciples from seeking positions of authority. They should humiliate themselves rather than exalt themselves. In Luke 22.24–27, Jesus exhorted his disciples to be slaves during the Last Supper, when he was about to demonstrate the most slavish act of his life: death by crucifixion, a torturous punishment used for slaves and barbarian rebels.

In John 13.3–17, Jesus demonstrated what slavery looked like by washing his disciples' feet. 'Very truly, I tell you, slaves are not greater than their master, nor are messengers greater than the one who sent them' (v 16). If Jesus lived like a slave, so should his followers.

If Jesus lived like a slave, so should his followers

In Phil 2.5–11, Paul described the incarnation with the language of enslavement. Paul said that Jesus did not exploit his equality with God, but emptied himself. And once he became human, Jesus humbled (or humiliated) himself by the ultimate obedience when he died on a Roman cross. For Jesus, becoming human meant becoming a slave. Because of this radical obedience, God exalted Jesus, restoring his original status.

Paul identified himself as a slave (Rom 1.1; Phil 1.1). He gave up his own status and privilege for the sake of others, as Jesus expected his disciples to do (1 Cor 9.19). Paul claimed that, because he identified himself as a slave, some people could not understand the gospel he preached (2 Cor 4.5). Like a slave, Paul was beaten, dishonoured and disregarded. Because of his willing enslavement to God, the gospel and his churches, Paul experienced the shame of slavery in the Roman Empire.

Back in Phil 2.5–11, Paul's celebration of Jesus's willing enslavement had clear implications for the Philippian Christians. They should imitate Jesus by placing others above themselves:

> Do nothing from selfish ambition or conceit, but in humility regard others as better than yourselves. Let each of you look not to your own interests, but to the interests of others. Let the same mind be in you that was in Christ Jesus. (Phil 2.4–5)

As we have seen, slaves in Roman society had no personal rights or privileges. They were unable to maintain personal, bodily boundaries. From the slave owners' perspective, slaves existed for their benefit and pleasure. Paul's exhortation for Christians to be slaves reflected these attributes of slavery (see also Gal 5.13–14 and 1 Pet 2.16).

Jesus, Paul and Peter all expected leaders in the church and ordinary Christians to be obedient to God and to submit to each other like slaves. What would this mean for different members of the early church?

Slaves were already obedient and submissive to their owners, so on the surface the expectation of mutual slavery in the church would not seem different from their everyday lives. However, the declaration of freedom in Christ changed slaves' essential identity. If slaves are, in fact, free in Christ, then they get to choose to enslave themselves to their sisters and brothers in the church—just as Jesus himself did

What about slave owners? The call to become like slaves, put others' needs ahead of their own and regard others as better than themselves deeply challenged the power and authority of a slave owner. If 'there is no longer slave or free' in Christ, then slaves and slave owners had the same identity—and it was not the identity of the owner, but the slave (Gal 3.28).

What might it mean to give up privilege and identify with the powerless?

The New Testament teaching to be like slaves flattened the Roman hierarchy by taking social privilege away from slave owners (as well as fathers, husbands, the wealthy and even the twelve disciples in the gospels and Eph 5.21–6.4; Col 3.18–21; Jas 2.1–9; 1 Pet 3.7). This challenge to people with social power or prestige is difficult to hear and to live out. Who are the people with privilege and power in our communities? What might it mean to give up such privilege and identify with the powerless as we seek to imitate Christ?

Sin and Slavery, Freedom and Grace

> Do you not know that if you present yourselves to anyone as obedient slaves, you are slaves of the one whom you obey, either of sin, which leads to death, or of obedience, which leads to righteousness? But thanks be to God that you, having once been slaves of sin, have become

> obedient from the heart to the form of teaching to which you were entrusted, and that you, having been set free from sin, have become slaves of righteousness. (Rom 6.16–18)

The metaphor of slavery and freedom runs through Rom 5–8. The Christians in Rome lived at the centre of the imperial slave society. Roman Italy had the highest percentage of slaves of any region of the Empire.[49] Paul's metaphors in his letter to the Roman churches used the reality they knew to teach a powerful lesson about sin, death, grace and life.

For Paul, sin and death began to rule the world as soon as Adam disobeyed God (Rom 5.12–17).[50] Everyone in the world from Adam onwards lived in the kingdom of sin and death. The idea of dominion is developed into a metaphor of slavery in Rom 6.5–23. If sin ruled the world, then sin enslaved the world. Paul argued that humanity and creation itself were caught in 'bondage to decay' (Rom 8.20–21). For humans, bondage meant that all people must obey sin, doing what their owner wants (Rom 6.6–7 and Rom 6.12–14). As slaves, humans had no other option!

The most common way out of slavery in the Roman Empire was death, and Paul said that only through death can a person be freed from the ownership of sin and death. Paul had one particular death in mind in Rom 6.1–11. In his crucifixion and resurrection, Jesus broke the power of sin and death over the world. Christians who are crucified with Christ share in the victory of Christ over sin and death.

> So you also must consider yourselves dead to sin and alive to God in Christ Jesus. (Rom 6.11)

Freedom from sin did not mean Christians had no owner. In Christ, they were slaves to God, obedient to righteousness, and rewarded with life (Rom 6.13–23). For an audience in the heart of the Roman Empire, the metaphors of slavery and freedom, death and life, would resonate with slaves and slave owners alike. But as in the mutual enslavement of Christians to each other, the call to be slaves to God reminded slave owners that they also were owned. As Paul said in 1 Cor 6.19–20, no one belonged to themself. Christians were purchased by God, and like slaves they should live for God.

5

Conclusions

Slavery was (and is) a brutal, dehumanizing institution. Even if some Roman slaves had relatively comfortable lives, those lives belonged to someone else. The lack of legal rights and privileges, the inability to exercise control over one's own body, and the daily humiliations and abuses of enslavement were a burden. This was the experience for many people we meet in the stories and letters of the New Testament.

In the Gospels and Acts, we see close relationships between slave owners and slaves, including the centurion's slave in Capernaum, the slave Rhoda in Acts, and the slaves baptized with their owners' households in Acts. Jesus' parables drew on real expectations for slaves' lives: obedience to the owner; the benefits the owner receives from slavery; the casual brutality slaves experienced; and the potential for slaves to become wealthy and powerful as they exercised their owners' power.

Instructions given to slaves in the letters of Paul and Peter reflected the social limitations on slaves. They also provided slaves with a way to resist by placing true ownership with God. Slave owners were cautioned to remember that they were also slaves, and should treat their slaves accordingly. 'As slaves of God, live as free people' (1 Pet 2.16); Peter's instruction expressed the tension of the presence of slaves and slave owners in the church.

The consistent refrain of willing enslavement and submission challenged Roman social norms

For those of us who live in societies that have declared slavery to be illegal, it can be difficult to understand why Jesus, Paul or others in the early church did not call for an end to the system of slavery. But although no New Testament text told slave owners to free their slaves, the consistent refrain of willing enslavement and submission to others challenged Roman social norms. The witness of Christians to the equality of slaves and slave owners in Christ embodied the new creation, even though the fallen creation with its emphasis on power and status lingered on (see 2 Cor 5.16–17; Gal 3.27–29 and Col 3.10–11).

The New Testament reflected its historical, social and cultural contexts, including Rome's slave society. In this particular context, the demand for those who sought positions of power, privilege, and status within the Christian community to be slaves struck a radical note. That all Christians should submit to each other, putting the needs of others ahead of their own rights, challenged the Roman definition of humanity around self-control, power over others and honour. The shock of this message still reverberates today, if we let it.

For Further Reading

Keith Bradley, *Slavery and Society at Rome* (Cambridge University Press, 1994). I highly recommend Bradley for a thorough, thoughtful introduction to the realities and rhetoric of the Roman system of slavery.

Allen Callahan, *The Talking Book: African Americans and the Bible* (New Haven, CT: Yale University Press, 2006). Callahan explores the ways the New Testament was used to oppress slaves in the United States, and also the ways that African Americans have used the New Testament to challenge systems of slavery and oppression. He also addresses the significance of the Bible within African American traditions.

Jennifer Glancy, *Slavery in Early Christianity* (Minneapolis, MN: Fortress, 2006). Glancy's book addresses the harsh realities of slavery in the Roman world. Her challenging work offers a critical, unsettling interpretation of slavery in the New Testament.

Murray J Harris, *Slave of Christ: A New Testament Metaphor for Total Devotion to Christ*, New Studies in Biblical Theology 8 (Leicester: Apollos, 1999). Harris discusses the references to slavery in the New Testament both as a reflection of the realities of slavery and as a metaphor for Christian commitment to Jesus.

Matthew Johnson, Noel James and Demetrius Williams (eds), *Onesimus Our Brother: Reading Religion, Race, and Culture in Philemon* (Minneapolis, MN: Fortress, 2012). This collection of essays by African American scholars explores many different interpretations of Philemon—and much more. The authors discuss the history of slavery in the United States, race and racism in the church, and how New Testament texts speak into these concerns.

Jo-Ann Shelton, *As the Romans Did* (Oxford University Press, 1998). This book collects a variety of texts written by the peoples of the Roman Empire. It gives a great introduction to what life was like in the time of the New Testament.

Notes

1 K Bradley, *Slavery and Society at Rome* (Cambridge University Press, 1994) pp 12–16, and N Morley, 'Slavery Under the Principate' in K Bradley and P Cartledge (eds), *The Cambridge World History of Slavery, Volume 1: The Ancient Mediterranean World* (Cambridge University Press, 2011) pp 265–286, here p 284.

2 Bradley, *Slavery, op cit*, pp 10–12; W Scheidel, 'The Roman Slave Supply' in *The Cambridge World History, op cit*, pp 287–310, here pp 288–292.

3 Scheidel, 'Slave Supply,' *op cit*, pp 299–300.

4 J Glancy, *Slavery in Early Christianity* (Minneapolis, MN: Fortress, 2006) pp 10–11.

5 Scheidel, 'Slave Supply,' *op cit*, pp 300–304.

6 Bradley, *Slavery, op cit*, pp 12–15.

7 L Foxhall, *Studying Gender in Classical Antiquity* (Cambridge University Press, 2013) pp 68–113.

8 See Bradley, *Slavery, op cit*, p 24 and Morley, 'Slavery,' *op cit*, pp 280–283.

9 Bradley, *Slavery, op cit*, p 181.

10 Bradley, *Slavery, op cit*, pp 25–26.

11 The websites perseus.tufts.edu and penelope.uchicago.edu/Thayer/ have many texts in translation.

12 M Lefkowitz and M Fant, *Women's Life in Greece and Rome* (Baltimore, MD: Johns Hopkins University Press, 2005); J Shelton, *As the Romans Did* (Oxford University Press, 1998); and T Wiedemann, *Greek and Roman Slavery* (London: Routledge, 2005).

13 The first quotation is Inscriptiones Latinae Selectae 1519, and the second is Corpus Inscriptionum Latinarum 6.9980.

14 See also Bradley, *Slavery, op cit*, p 27 and Glancy, *Slavery, op cit*, pp 77–78.

15 Bradley, *Slavery, op cit*, pp 37–38.

16 Bradley, *Slavery, op cit*, p 35 and Glancy, *Slavery, op cit*, pp 74–77.

17 Bradley, *Slavery, op cit*, p 34.

18 See C Laes, 'Desperately Different? *Delicia* Children in the Roman Household' in D Balch and C Osiek (eds), *Early Christian Families in Context* (Grand Rapids, MI: Eerdmans, 2003) pp 298–324, especially pp 300–304.

19 Glancy, *Slavery, op cit*, pp 18–19.

20 P duBois, *Slavery: Antiquity and Its Legacy* (Oxford University Press, 2009) pp 1–17.

21 Glancy, *Slavery, op cit*, p 45; Bradley, *Slavery, op cit*, pp 84–85.

22 Bradley, *Slavery, op cit*, pp 87–88.

23 Bradley, *Slavery, op cit*, pp 86–87.

24 Bradley, *Slavery, op cit*, pp 50–51.

25 Glancy, *Slavery, op cit*, pp 50–57.

26 Glancy, *Slavery, op cit*, pp 58–70.

27 See M Harris, *Slave of Christ: A New Testament Metaphor for Total Devotion to Christ* (Leicester: Apollos, 1999) p 54.

28 Bradley, *Slavery, op cit*, pp 135–139, discusses Stoic views on slavery.

29 This inscription from the third century BC can be found in Lefkowitz and Fant, *Women's Life, op cit*, p 379.

30 Bradley, *Slavery, op cit*, p 155.

31 Bradley, *Slavery, op cit*, pp 25, 155–160.

32 Quoted in Wiedemann, *Slavery, op cit*, pp 46–47.

33 Bradley, *Slavery, op cit*, pp 160–62. See also Glancy, *Slavery, op cit*, pp 94–95.

34 Bradley, *Slavery, op cit*, pp 118–121.

35 Glancy, *Slavery, op cit*, pp 88–90.

36 See also Bradley, *Slavery, op cit*, pp 112–115.

37 A Thiselton, *The First Epistle to the Corinthians: A Commentary on the Greek Text* (Grand Rapids, MI: Eerdmans, 2000) pp 553-562, analyzes the different interpretations.

38 M Johnson, J Noel, and D Williams (eds), *Onesimus Our Brother: Reading Religion, Race, and Culture in Philemon* (Minneapolis, MN: Fortress, 2012) cover the interpretations discussed here (and other options).

39 P Gooder, *Phoebe* (Downers Grove, IL: InterVarsity Press, 2018) explores this tension in a novel based on the life of Phoebe (Rom 16.1-4).

40 Supporters of slavery also emphasized slave owners in biblical narratives, the laws concerning slavery in Exodus and Deuteronomy, and Gen 9.24–27 to justify their position.

41 A Callahan, *The Talking Book: African Americans and the Bible* (New Haven, CT: Yale University Press, 2006) pp 21-39; duBois, *Slavery, op cit*, pp 69–75.

42 Callahan, *Talking Book, op cit*, pp 41-48; duBois, *Slavery, op cit*, pp 66–68.

43 Callahan, *Talking Book, op cit*, p xiii.

44 Some scholars argue this challenge should lead to the end of slavery as a system, as seems to have been the case for some second-century churches. See C Martin, 'The Eyes Have It: Slaves in the Communities of Christ-Believers' in R Horsley (ed), *A People's History of Christianity, Volume 1: Christian Origins* (Minneapolis, MN: Fortress, 2005) pp 221-239, especially pp 229-236.

45 Bradley, *Slavery, op cit*, p 27.

46 C Reeder, 'Child, Children,' in J Green (ed), *Dictionary of Jesus and the Gospels* (Downers Grove, IL: InterVarsity Press, 2013) pp 109-113.

47 C Conway, *Behold the Man* (Oxford University Press, 2008) pp 99–100.

48 Note that Jesus is described with the language of 'service' here (*diakonos, diakoneō*) rather than 'slavery' (*doulos, douleuō*). There is, however, a clear parallel between the enslavement of the disciples and the servanthood of Jesus.

49 Bradley, *Slavery, op cit*, p 12.

50 See B Gaventa, *When in Romans* (Grand Rapids, MI: Baker Academic, 2016) pp 34–46.